Improving Student Writing

Paragraphs

Jan Goldberg

Written by: Jan Goldberg
Edited by: Jessica Smuksta
Cover designed by: Alan Jansen
Interior designed by: Nicole Bjorgo and Kim Radke

© Learning Resources, Inc., Vernon Hills, Illinois (U.S.A.)
   Learning Resources Ltd., King's Lynn, Norfolk (U.K.)

All rights reserved. This book is copyrighted. No part of this book may be reproduced, stored in a retrieval system or transmitted, in any form or by any means electronic, mechanical, photocopying, recording or otherwise, without written permission, except for the specific permission stated below.

Each blackline master is intended for reproduction in quantities sufficient for classroom use. Permission is granted to the purchaser to reproduce each blackline master in quantities suitable for noncommercial classroom use.

ISBN: 1-56911-528-1

Printed in China

Contents

Introduction 4

UNIT ONE VOCABULARY

Synonyms, Antonyms, and Homophones 5
Analogies 6

UNIT TWO SHAPING SOLID SENTENCES

Subjects and Predicates 7
Types of Sentences: Declarative and Interrogative Sentences 8
Types of Sentences: Imperative and Exclamatory Sentences 9
Scrambled Sentences 10

UNIT THREE GRAMMAR AND USAGE

Nouns 11
Pronouns 12
Verbs 13
Verb Tenses 14
Adjectives 15
Adverbs 16
Prepositions and Prepositional Phrases 17
Direct Objects 18
Conjunctions: Compound Sentences 19
Interjections 20
Dialogue: Conversation 21

UNIT FOUR CREATIVE WRITING

Appositives 22
Main Ideas 23
Topic Sentences 24
Sentences and Paragraphs 25
Paragraphs 26
Paragraph Order 27
The Writing Process 28
Author's Purpose: To Persuade, Inform, or Entertain 29
Characterization, Setting, and Plot 30
Leads (Beginnings) and Endings 31
Show, Don't Tell! 32
Figures of Speech 33
Fact or Opinion 34
Descriptive Writing 35
Expository Writing 36
5 Ws and an H 37
Narrative Writing 38
Friendly Letters 39
Poetry 40

Improving Student Writing: **Paragraphs**

One of the highest goals we have for our children is that they learn to communicate their ideas effectively both verbally and in writing. This series is designed to help students achieve this goal. Parents and teachers can work together to promote this process.

The worksheets in this book are ideal for both home and classroom use. They are intended to reinforce and extend basic writing concepts. Research shows us that mastery of skills comes with exposure and drill. To be internalized, concepts must be reviewed until they become second nature.

The lessons are organized around a series of units. They are arranged in a logical sequence progressing from vocabulary and sentences to grammar and usage. The book concludes with exercises in composition. Writing original sentences and stories is also emphasized.

Teachers can use these activities as part of whatever writing program they favor. Lessons can be done individually or as a group. Educators who work with ESL/EFL students will find the series particularly valuable in providing easy-to-understand writing activities to help students master the basics of the English language.

Note the book's following features:
- Easy-to-understand directions
- Age-appropriate activities that reinforce writing skills
- A variety of writing activities to create interest and spark creativity
- A color-coded, self-checking answer key for the overhead

How to Use the Answer Key with an Overhead Projector

The four overhead pages provide answers for the Part One sections of each worksheet. Detach the overhead sheets and the overhead viewing tool at their perforated edge, and store them in the back cover pocket when they are not in use.

When you want to show a particular worksheet's answers, find that page number on one of the four overhead sheets. Slide the overhead sheet into the overhead viewing tool horizontally so that the answer key is showing in the open rectangle. Note that the answers for page 39 are printed on the last overhead transparency, which should be placed directly on the overhead projector.

Notice that most words in the Answer Key are color-coded by the part of speech they represent.

Part of speech		Color
nouns	=	green
pronouns	=	light green
verbs	=	yellow
adjectives	=	red
adverbs	=	orange
conjunctions	=	violet
prepositions	=	blue

Use the color-coded system to help teach your children how to recognize the parts of speech. Challenge them beyond the activities in this book by asking them to identify certain parts of speech in each exercise.

This color-coded system for the parts of speech matches the Learning Resources® Reading Rods® Overhead Language Sets and the Sentence Building Reading Rods® Kit. Combine this *Improving Student Writing* overhead instruction series with fun, hands-on Reading Rods® to create lifelong readers and writers!

UNIT ONE **VOCABULARY**

Name: _____

Synonyms, Antonyms, and Homophones

Part One

Decide how each of the words in Column A is related to the matching number in Column B. In Column C, put S for synonym, A for antonym, or H for homophone.

Column A	Column B	Column C
1) thrive	1) flourish	1) _____
2) cause	2) effect	2) _____
3) questionnaire	3) survey	3) _____
4) novice	4) amateur	4) _____
5) waste	5) waist	5) _____
6) audible	6) aloud	6) _____
7) through	7) threw	7) _____
8) gape	8) observe	8) _____
9) tough	9) easy	9) _____
10) flu	10) flew	10) _____

Tip Corner

A synonym is a word that has the same or similar meaning as another word.
Example: brilliant/genius

An antonym is a word that has the opposite meaning of another word.
Example: plentiful/scarce

A homophone is a word that sounds like another word or words but has a different spelling and/or meaning.
Example: right/write

Part Two

Create four of your own pairs of synonyms, antonyms, and homophones.

Synonyms   Antonyms   Homophones

_____ _____   _____ _____   _____ _____

_____ _____   _____ _____   _____ _____

_____ _____   _____ _____   _____ _____

_____ _____   _____ _____   _____ _____

UNIT ONE **VOCABULARY**

Name:_____

Analogies

Part One

Decide how each of the pairs of words below is related. Then write 1, 2, or 3 to indicate which of the types of analogies in the Tip Corner apply to that pair of words.

1) Walk is to run as stop is to go. ____

2) Toe is to foot as page is to book. ____

3) Teach is to educate as gloves are to mittens. ____

4) Ear is to head as gums are to mouth. ____

5) Excellent is to outstanding as gloomy is to sad. ____

6) Happy is to sad as white is to black. ____

7) Peace is to war as many is to none. ____

8) Kitchen is to house as eraser is to pencil. ____

9) Collar is to shirt as knob is to door. ____

10) Work is to play as win is to lose. ____

Tip Corner

An analogy specifies a relationship between two pairs of words. There are many types of analogies. Below are three.

Examples:
1) Part to whole: *Beak* is to *bird* as *tail* is to *cat*.
2) Antonym analogies: *Boy* is to *girl* as *up* is to *down*.
3) Synonym analogies: *Hot* is to *warm* as *small* is to *little*.

Part Two

Write three of each kind of analogy.

Part to whole: _____

_____

_____

Antonym analogies: _____

_____

_____

Synonym analogies: _____

_____

_____

UNIT TWO **SHAPING SOLID SENTENCES**

Name:_____

Subjects and Predicates

Part One

Circle each complete subject and underline every complete predicate in the sentences below.

1) The library closes earlier on Saturdays.

2) Our new assignment is a two-week weather project.

3) Emma and Grace wrote all 100 invitations.

4) The mailman delivered my tickets today.

5) The all-night rain created puddles everywhere.

6) He washed and polished his father's car for $5.00.

7) Wednesday is my favorite day of the week.

8) The noise is preventing me from concentrating on my homework.

9) Alexis barged right into the assembly hall without a pass.

10) Ryan and Michael were given a detention for fighting.

Tip Corner

The subject tells who or what a sentence is about. The predicate always includes a verb and tells what the subject does, did, or is doing.

In the example below, the complete subject is circled and the complete predicate is underlined.

Example: The black raincoat fell on the floor.

Part Two

Write ten sentences about winter. Circle the complete subjects and underline the complete predicates.

_____
_____
_____
_____
_____
_____
_____
_____
_____
_____

UNIT TWO **SHAPING SOLID SENTENCES**

Name:_____

Types of Sentences: **Declarative** and **Interrogative Sentences**

Part One

Read the following sentences and label them as declarative sentences (D) or interrogative sentences (I). Then add the correct punctuation.

1) Joshua and his family go out to dinner at least once each week _____

2) After the baseball game, he went to sleep on the sofa _____

3) How many packages did you mail at the post office _____

4) Jessica and Alyssa are going shopping at the mall today _____

5) What are you planning to wear to the party on Saturday night _____

6) The rain stopped for a while and then started up again later _____

7) How many cities will you be visiting on your trip next summer _____

8) We'd better tell Mr. Schabel, our science teacher, that we are almost out of computer paper _____

9) Can you pick up more computer paper when you are at the mall _____

10) Alyssa said that she would be happy to buy some computer paper _____

Tip Corner

Declarative sentences are statements that end with a period. **.**

Example:
Rachel knew she was doing something wrong.

Interrogative sentences are questions and therefore end with a question mark. **?**

Example:
Why would she have done that?

Part Two

Write a paragraph about the best gift you ever received. Label each sentence that is declarative (D) and each that is interrogative (I).

UNIT TWO **SHAPING SOLID SENTENCES**

Name:_____

Types of Sentences: Imperative and Exclamatory Sentences

Part One
Read the following sentences and decide if they are imperative or exclamatory. Put an *I* for imperatives or an *E* for exclamations. Then add the correct punctuation.

1) Blow out all your birthday candles _____

2) I can't believe he ate 44 hot dogs _____

3) That runaway train is going to jump the track _____

4) Study hard for the test on Friday _____

5) Write an article on storm damage for the school paper _____

6) He took my lunch money _____

7) Take out the garbage and sweep the sidewalk _____

8) Make sure you touch all of the bases _____

9) Open your book to page 79 _____

10) That tornado touched down ten miles from my house _____

Tip Corner

Imperative sentences are commands, sentences that give orders, requests, or instructions. Commands can end with either a period or an exclamation mark, depending on how forceful the command is.

Example:

Clean your room! **or** Clean your room.

Exclamations are sentences that display excitement or surprise. They end with exclamation marks.

Example:

The little boy disappeared!

Part Two
Write a story that includes a weather disaster. Include at least three imperative or exclamatory sentences. Identify each with an *I* or an *E*.

UNIT TWO **SHAPING SOLID SENTENCES**

Name:_____

Scrambled Sentences

Part One

Unscramble each of the sentences below. Then add the correct punctuation and capitalization.

1) desk the to belong this books Joshua on
_____

2) to of I game two friends with went the my
_____

3) dusted washed and floors the Dylan carpets the vacuumed
_____

4) the he story and on computer his edited wrote
_____

5) trimmed mowed the bushes Noah the and lawn then
_____

6) package Sarah to a used the scissors untie
_____

7) went sleep read to and the Brian then book
_____

8) followed the solved and he puzzle directions the
_____

9) day good miss of and Jesse school did grades not a received
_____

10) down his he drink he spilled fell when
_____

Tip Corner

Words in a sentence need to be in a logical order. Put the following scrambled sentences in the proper order.

Example:

last sleep I remember can't before I when 11:00 to went

I can't remember when I last went to sleep before 11:00.

Part Two

If you could travel in a time machine, would you like to go forward or back in time? Write a paragraph about your adventure.

UNIT THREE **GRAMMAR AND USAGE**

Name: _____

Nouns

Part One
Read the following underlined list of words and the sample sentences that use the words. Then circle all the nouns on the list.

Tip Corner
A noun is a word that names a person, place, or thing.

1) <u>abrasion</u>: Matthew's abrasion required medical treatment from a doctor.

2) <u>abrupt</u>: The abrupt stop made him spill his drink.

3) <u>bargain</u>: The radio was truly a bargain!

4) <u>citation</u>: Joshua's father received a citation for not stopping at the stop sign.

5) <u>equator</u>: The equator is a line around the middle of the earth.

6) <u>glossary</u>: If you don't know the meaning, look up the word in the glossary.

7) <u>hammock</u>: Chloe fell asleep in the hammock.

8) <u>injection</u>: The doctor had to give himself an injection.

9) <u>mild</u>: The experts are predicting that we will have a mild winter.

10) <u>presume</u>: From what you say, I presume that you don't want to attend the concert.

Part Two
Write a story using at least three of the nouns you circled.

_____
_____
_____
_____
_____
_____
_____
_____
_____

UNIT THREE **GRAMMAR AND USAGE**

Name:_____

Pronouns

Part One

Choose the correct pronoun from the Pronoun Box to complete each sentence correctly. Then identify which kind of pronoun it is—nominative, objective, or possessive. Label the pronoun with an *N* for nominative, *O* for objective, or *P* for possessive.

Pronoun Box						
he	she	it	them	us	his	your

1) Mom asked _____ to clean our rooms after school.

2) They didn't know how long it would take for _____ to clean up.

3) _____ knew that his dog was well-behaved and wouldn't disturb anything.

4) Jonathon is going to take _____ cat with him on the trip.

5) You should check with _____ mom before you sign up.

6) _____ tripped on her new rug and _____ tore as she fell.

Part Two

If you could pretend to be any kind of transportation, what would you be—a train, a fast car, a boat, a bus, or something else? Why would you make that choice? Describe what you look like and what you do. Concentrate on the pronouns you use in your paragraph. Circle them and identify their type by using *N*, *O*, or *P*.

Tip Corner

A pronoun is a word that is used in place of a noun. The noun that the pronoun replaces is called the antecedent.

Example:
Joslyn is a fifth grade student. She has a straight A average.

Joslyn = proper noun
She = pronoun
Joslyn = antecedent

There are three types of pronouns:

Subject pronouns (Nominative)
A subject pronoun takes the place of a noun or nouns in the subject of a sentence.

Example:
Joanna and Brian will work on the project. **(They)** will work on the project.

Object pronouns (Objective)
An object pronoun takes the place of a noun or nouns in the predicate of a sentence.

Example:
Brian's mother will take (Brian and Joanna) to the library to study.
Brian's mother will take **(them)** to the library to study.

Possessive pronouns (Possessive)
A possessive pronoun shows ownership. Some possessive pronouns take the place of nouns.

Example:
Brian's mother will help Brian and Joanna with (their) books

UNIT THREE **GRAMMAR AND USAGE**

Name:_____

Verbs

Part One

Read the following sentences. Circle the helping verbs and underline the main verbs.

1) Her mother was carrying in the groceries.
2) Mary will read her magazine on the porch.
3) Will she complete her project on time?
4) I am planning on being on time for work tomorrow.
5) Mary's brother has answered the phone three times.
6) My father was driving me to the mall when we saw the accident.
7) Sherri is talking on the phone.
8) I have washed my face and brushed my hair.
9) The light bulb is cracking under the weight of the lamp.
10) John will walk the dog every night.

Tip Corner

A verb is a word or group of words that expresses action or a state of being. The main verb is the one that states the action. Helping verbs are words like *am*, *is*, *was*, or *has* that help to convey the time the action was completed. They may be separated from the main verb.

Example:
Pedro was skating on the lake.

Part Two

Write a story about what you would invent to make life better. Underline helping verbs and circle main verbs.

_____
_____
_____
_____
_____
_____
_____
_____
_____

UNIT THREE **GRAMMAR AND USAGE**

Name: _____

Verb Tenses

Part One

Fill in the blanks with the requested form of the word specified.

1) I _____ a glass every day. (present tense of use)

2) I _____ a glass yesterday. (past tense of use)

3) I _____ I should be made captain. (present tense of think)

4) I _____ I would be named captain. (past tense of think)

5) I _____ how well everyone treats me. (present tense of appreciate)

6) I _____ how everyone treated me at my previous school. (past tense of appreciate)

7) I _____ when I don't know what else to do. (present tense of complain)

8) I _____ about it yesterday, but no one listened. (past tense of complain)

9) I _____ anyone who lies. (present tense of dislike)

10) I _____ him from the minute I met him. (past tense of dislike)

Tip Corner

Tenses of verbs tell whether an action or state of being took place in the past, in the present, or in the future. We use the past tense of a verb to point to something that happened in the past. The simple past tense consists of one word that describes a past action. Many verbs form the simple past tense by adding *d* or *ed* to the present tense.

Example:
Today we jump.
Yesterday we jumped.

Other verbs form the simple past tense irregularly. The spelling is sometimes considerably different from the present tense spelling of the same verb.

Example:
Today we buy bread.
Yesterday we bought bread.
Today we cut the logs.
Yesterday we cut the logs.

Part Two

Write a paragraph describing the best advice anyone ever gave you. Be sure to use the correct tense of the verbs you include. Indicate *PR* for present tense verbs and *PT* for past tense verbs. Use *F* for future tense verbs.

UNIT THREE **GRAMMAR AND USAGE**

Name:_____

Adjectives

Part One

Read each sentence and underline every adjective. Then decide which question the adjective answers and write above it HW for *how many* and WK for *what kind*.

1) I've never seen a smaller kitten with such stark white fur.

2) No matter what, Barclay is always able to find his favorite yellow ball.

3) Sherri hated fishing until she caught several weighty, unidentified fish.

4) Dogs give people an immeasurable amount of joy.

5) July is always a very hot, oppressive month.

6) I very much enjoy the longer days of summer.

7) You should always take large amounts of photos when on vacation.

8) Even though Jeremy hit the winning shot, he was not given a starting position.

9) When the new baby is in the room, the Labrador retriever must stay out.

10) If you want to help her cook the twenty-pound turkey, bring the over-sized aluminum pan.

Tip Corner

Adjectives modify nouns or pronouns. They answer the questions *how many* and *what kind*. An adjective usually comes before the noun or the pronoun that it modifies.

Example:

My cousin bought a *new multi-purpose* radio to replace the one she lost.

Both *new* and *multi-purpose* tell what kind of radio she bought.

Part Two

If you were an animal, what would you choose to be? Pretending that you are that animal, describe where you live, what you eat, who your friends are, and who your enemies are. Be sure to use specific adjectives to make your writing more descriptive and more interesting. Circle all the adjectives.

UNIT THREE **GRAMMAR AND USAGE**

Name: _____

Adverbs

Part One

Read each sentence and fill in the chart below.

1) Taylor raced outside to catch up with his friends.

2) I carefully planted the flowers in the garden.

3) The mother delicately touched her baby's face.

4) Ashley will gladly skate at the rink this afternoon.

5) Mother slowly lifted her broken leg off the ground.

6) Noah spoke firmly when he gave his presidential speech.

7) Emily sprinted happily across the park and on to the party.

8) Kayla often accepts all extra credit assignments.

9) Once all of the children had gathered safely, the festivities could begin.

10) Chloe never wore her blue ribbon.

Tip Corner

Adverbs describe verbs. They express how, when, and where things happen.

Example:
The doctor says that my elbow will heal naturally.

Naturally = adverb (expressing how)

	Adverb	Word It Modifies	Question Answered
1)			
2)			
3)			
4)			
5)			
6)			
7)			
8)			
9)			
10)			

Part Two

Write a paragraph or two about something that really bothers you. Include at least three adverbs. Then create and fill in a chart like the one above.

UNIT THREE **GRAMMAR AND USAGE**

Name:_____

Prepositions and Prepositional Phrases

Part One

Read each sentence below and write the prepositional phrase on the line provided. Write whether the phrase is being used as an adjective (adj.) or adverb (adv.).

1) Jason was afraid to go across the river.
_____

2) How far do you live from the school?
_____

3) His family took a long trip around the United States.
_____

4) We live in the house on the corner.
_____

5) The toddler likes to sleep with the light on.
_____

6) The old car coughed and broke down on the hill.
_____

7) You could see the garden in the back yard.
_____

8) The bicycle stand was placed before the railroad tracks. _____

9) Stay away from the street! _____

10) Sheri went to the store to buy new sneakers.
_____

Tip Corner

Prepositions are words that show the relation of the noun following it to another word in the sentence. Prepositions include *with, on, for, after, at, by, in, against, instead, of, near,* and *between*. The noun after the preposition is the object of the preposition. A prepositional phrase is a preposition, its object, and any words that describe the object. These phrases are used like adjectives and adverbs. A good way to check if you have correctly identified the prepositional phrase is to see if the sentence still makes sense without it.

Example:

The boy <u>with the leg brace</u> entered last. The prepositional phrase is used here as an adjective. It modifies or further describes the noun *boy*.

Example:

The young girl ran <u>between the aisles</u>. The prepositional phrase is used here as an adverb. It modifies or further describes the verb *ran*.

Part Two

Pretend that you are the principal of your school. What policies or procedures would you like to change? Write several paragraphs on this topic. Be sure to use prepositional phrases correctly. Circle the prepositions. Then underline the prepositional phrases and indicate whether they are being used as adjectives or adverbs.

UNIT THREE **GRAMMAR AND USAGE**

Name: _____

Direct Objects

Part One

Read the following sentences and underline the subject, circle the verb, and put two lines underneath the direct objects.

1) Taylor wrapped the birthday present.

2) I bought a cage for our new hamster.

3) The doctor examined me in his office.

4) Debbie baked a chocolate cake with sprinkles.

5) She did not have enough milk for breakfast.

6) The class entertained all of the parents.

7) Kayla sent Madison a birthday card.

8) Noah told me a funny story.

9) I bought a magazine at the store.

10) The whole family watched television together.

Tip Corner

The subject of a sentence tells who or what the sentence is about. The word that pinpoints what the subject did or is doing is the verb. In many cases, there is a noun after the verb that names the object or person who received the action. This word is called the direct object.

Example:

The teacher handed the book to me.

The teacher = complete subject

handed = verb

book = direct object

Part Two

Write a paragraph or two about your favorite television show. Why do you like it? Then label all of the subjects, verbs, and direct objects.

_____
_____
_____
_____
_____
_____
_____

UNIT THREE **GRAMMAR AND USAGE**

Name:_____

Conjunctions: **Compound Sentences**

Part One

Which of the following sentences contain two independent clauses? Put an *X* after the sentences that do. Circle the conjunctions in these compound sentences.

1) John lived in England but he considered himself a native of the United States. _____

2) The storm produced high winds and it caused flooding in the lowlands. _____

3) Carol and Sue had to decide about cooking dinner or going out to eat. _____

4) The teacher and the principal scolded Bruce for missing school. _____

5) Bill went to school to learn to read and write. _____

6) Michael hit a homer to win the game and then he smiled for hours. _____

7) The doctor said Ryan had a broken arm and two broken fingers. _____

8) Sarah went to the movies, ate popcorn, and drank coke. _____

9) Alexis got all As but she got a C in physical education. _____

10) Mother said Emily could do her homework or she could help plant flowers. _____

Tip Corner

A compound sentence is made up of two or more independent clauses. That means that each is a complete sentence. (Remember that a sentence can be simple even when it has a compound subject or predicate, or both.)

Clauses may be joined by using a comma and a conjunction. The words *and*, *but*, and *or* are the most commonly used conjunctions. *Yet*, *before*, *so*, *for*, and *nor* are also conjunctions.

Example:

Tina walked around in the park *before* she went to meet her mother.

This compound sentence is made up of two independent clauses. Each is a complete sentence.

Part Two

If you could meet anyone who lived in earlier times, whom would you choose? Write a paragraph about why you would choose that person. Include at least two compound sentences and use a conjunction.

UNIT THREE **GRAMMAR AND USAGE**

Name: _____

Interjections

Part One

Which of the following could be considered interjections?

1) Sorry. _____

2) Hey! _____

3) The boy answered. _____

4) Quick. _____

5) I won the contest. _____

6) Yes. _____

7) I won't ask for the time off. _____

8) Hurray! _____

9) My answer is no. _____

10) Oh no! _____

Tip Corner

Interjections are words or phrases that express feeling. They are thrown into a sentence and don't necessarily have any connection to the rest of the sentence. The actual word that is thrown in is the interjection. Always separate the interjection from the rest of the sentence with some punctuation mark. (Hint: Capitalize the first word of the sentence after the mark of end punctuation, such as a period, a question mark, or an exclamation point.)

Example:

Please hurry! The train is coming.

Part Two

Take each of the above that you checked off as being an interjection and write a sentence to go along with it. Then add an interjection to each sentence above that did not have one.

_____
_____
_____
_____
_____
_____
_____

Dialogue: **Conversation**

Part One
Read the following paragraph and make the necessary corrections according to the guidelines in the Tip Corner.

    I know what I'm going to do next summer said Juan. What are your plans asked Ramón. I'm going to offer an errand service to the neighborhood residents. There's a huge supermarket just down the street from my house, in addition to a post office, and some other stores. I can either walk to the shopping area or ride back and forth on my bicycle. I figure that while helping others I can make some money to put away for college. Sounds like a winning combination said Ramón.

Tip Corner
When including conversations in your writing, you need to (1) place quotation marks around each quote, (2) use words like *said* or *asked* with each quote (unless it is obvious who is speaking), and (3) begin a new paragraph for each quote.

Example:
"No, I won't do that," said Brittany.

Part Two
Write your own story and include some conversation between two characters.

_____
_____
_____
_____
_____
_____
_____
_____
_____
_____
_____
_____
_____

UNIT FOUR **CREATIVE WRITING**

Name:_____

Appositives

Part One

Read each sentence and underline the appositives. Some sentences have them and some don't. Put an X after the sentences that have an appositive.

1) Henry, the full-time gardener, trimmed the tree. _____

2) *Home and Away*, a travel magazine, is very interesting. _____

3) John was sleeping and then he woke up. _____

4) Dr. Olsen, my old doctor, just examined me. _____

5) My old friend and classmate was elected chairman. _____

6) Brett, my favorite cousin, was awakened by the phone. _____

7) Toni, a friend and neighbor, takes care of Barclay. _____

8) Mr. Jackson, our accountant, has an office downtown. _____

9) The town newspaper includes an early edition and a late edition. _____

10) The car, a shiny red convertible, comes equipped with two spare tires. _____

Tip Corner

An appositive is a group of words that follows a noun and describes it.

Example: Mr. Pointer, the school janitor, is always willing to help.

Part Two

Write a story beginning "I wish all children would . . ." and include at least three appositives.

_____
_____
_____
_____
_____
_____

UNIT FOUR **CREATIVE WRITING**

Name:_____

Main Ideas

Part One
Read the paragraph below and circle one of the following sentences that best summarizes the main point of this paragraph.

    Spunky came to live with us when I was five years old. He was so little we could hold him in the palm of our hands. A little black and white ball of fur, Spunky offered us unconditional love. Of course, of all members in the family, I was his favorite. He followed me around from room to room, hoping I would stop to scratch his head or offer some playtime. Of course, I often did. He was my favorite toy!

1) Spunky was the smallest dog we had ever seen.

2) Spunky and the author had a special bond of love.

3) All of the members of the family fought over Spunky.

4) We had Spunky for a long time.

5) Spunky had very soft fur.

Tip Corner
The subject of a paragraph is its main idea. After you read a paragraph, ask yourself questions like the following. What have you learned from reading this paragraph? Who or what was the paragraph about?

Part Two
Write a fantasy story about you and another character in danger. The other character could be a human, a non-human, or an animal.

_____
_____
_____
_____
_____
_____
_____
_____

UNIT FOUR **CREATIVE WRITING**

Name: _____

Topic Sentences

Part One

Alison is writing a story about how much she values the relationship she has with her mom. Her topic sentence is "My mom is the most amazing person I know."

Which of the following sentences supports this topic sentence?

1) She is intelligent and caring and always there for me.

2) Roses are her favorite flower.

3) I know I can always go to her for advice and help.

4) On Wednesdays, she does the shopping.

5) She was born in Indianapolis, Indiana.

6) We don't always agree on everything, but she is always willing to listen to my point of view.

7) Her sister, my aunt, lives in Florida.

Tip Corner

The topic sentence introduces the subject and tells what the paragraph will be about. Supporting details are provided by one or more sentences that give facts or additional information about the subject.

Part Two

Write a paragraph about someone you have a special relationship with. Be sure to include a topic sentence and supporting sentences that provide facts or additional information about the subject. End with a conclusion—a sentence that ends the paragraph and gives a summary, opinion, or something for the reader to think about.

_____
_____
_____
_____
_____
_____

UNIT FOUR **CREATIVE WRITING**

Name:_____

Sentences and Paragraphs

Part One

Below is a paragraph about tennis that has been broken down into sentences. Read the sentences and place them in the proper sequence to make a paragraph that reads logically and makes sense. Number each sentence (1–6) as each should be placed in the paragraph.

1) But, as you get better, you'll have more control over where the balls go.

2) This definitely makes the game more fun.

3) When you are a beginner, you'll be chasing many balls that fly everywhere.

4) Tennis offers great exercise and provides a new way to challenge yourself, both physically and mentally.

5) Tennis is a fun game that almost everyone can play!

6) Find a partner and grab a couple of tennis racquets and several cans of balls.

Tip Corner

A paragraph is a group of sentences that all focus on one subject. Sentences that are not about that subject should be placed in another paragraph.

Part Two

Write a paragraph about the sport you like to play most.

_____
_____
_____
_____
_____
_____
_____
_____
_____
_____

UNIT FOUR **CREATIVE WRITING**

Name: _____

Paragraphs

Part One

Below you will find a story with the paragraphs running together. Read the story and decide which sentences should begin new paragraphs. In the space below, number the paragraphs as they should be and indicate which sentences belong in which paragraphs. (You may have spaces left over.)

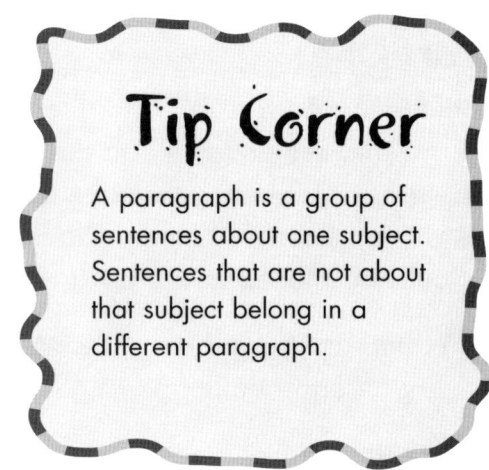

Tip Corner

A paragraph is a group of sentences about one subject. Sentences that are not about that subject belong in a different paragraph.

(1) When Sarah woke up that morning, she knew she didn't feel right. (2) She couldn't put her finger on what was bothering her. (3) Then she remembered. (4) "Today are the tryouts for the school play," she thought. (5) "Should I try out?" (6)"Her head said yes, but her stomach said no." (7) When Sarah got to school, everyone was talking about the school play. (8) Her best friend, Madison, was going to try out for a voice solo. (9) Sarah was sure Madison would make it. (10) Everyone knew Madison was very talented musically. (11) Sarah had never tried to do any kind of acting, but somehow she felt that she might like to try. (12) "Is there anything wrong with trying?" she said out loud to no one special. (13) When Mr. Miller the math teacher called on Sarah for an answer to a word problem, Sarah's mind was somewhere else. (14) When Mrs. Johnson asked her how many adjectives were in a sentence, her mind was somewhere else. (15) When her friends spoke to her, her mind was somewhere else. (16) Finally, it was 3:00—time for the tryouts. (17) Sarah couldn't consider the situation any longer. (18) It was decision time. (19) And, yes indeed, she had made hers!

Paragraph # _____ Sentences # _____
Paragraph # _____ Sentences # _____
Paragraph # _____ Sentences # _____
Paragraph # _____ Sentences # _____
Paragraph # _____ Sentences # _____
Paragraph # _____ Sentences # _____

Part Two

Write a story about a time when you had to make an important decision. Be sure to begin new paragraphs when you change subjects. End with a conclusion—a sentence that ends the paragraph and gives a summary, opinion, or something for the reader to think about.

UNIT FOUR **CREATIVE WRITING**

Name:_____

Paragraph Order

Part One

Some of the paragraphs that make up the story below are not in the correct order. Read the paragraphs and decide how they should be placed. Then put the paragraph numbers in the correct order.

1) Kayla gathered some shampoo and several large towels and walked outside. She looked around but didn't see Elijah or Rags. "Where could they be?" she thought. As she began to walk around the front, she caught sight of something whizzing through the back yard.

2) "Grab him," said Elijah! Kayla moved too slowly and Rags ran around the front.

3) "Let's corner him in the front yard," said Kayla.

4) "OK," said Elijah. But Rags was much too quick for the brother-and-sister-washing team.

5) Elijah and Kayla decided that today was the day. Their dog, Rags, was looking pretty gray and dingy. He didn't smell very good either. So, a bath was in order!

6) Finally, they noticed something stir behind the bushes. Slowly, they inched their way towards that area. "Aha," said Elijah. "We got you, Rags." So Rags decided to cooperate. He wasn't exactly a willing participant, but he did manage to stay still long enough for Elijah and Kayla to make his coat shiny and smelling fresh!

7) The two decided that they would split the responsibilities. Kayla would gather the items they would need and Elijah would set everything up. Then, they would meet outside where they had a huge metal basin suitable for washing Rags.

Tip Corner

Paragraphs in a story need to be in a logical sequence. Sometimes, you can tell the order by ascertaining events in order of time. Also, words like *first*, *then*, *next*, and *finally* are often used to help signal an order that is sensible.

Part Two

Write a story that features a pet you or someone you know has. Are your paragraphs in the correct order?

UNIT FOUR **CREATIVE WRITING**

Name:_____

The Writing Process

Part One

Following are a number of activities you might pursue in the process of creating a piece of writing. Which phase of the Writing Process would each activity fit into? Refer to the numbered phrases in the Tip Corner. (Be aware that even professional writers go back and forth among the phases as they are working on a writing project.)

1) Searching for spelling errors _____
2) Interviewing an expert on your topic _____
3) Choosing an idea to write about _____
4) Taking notes on a movie about your topic _____
5) Reading magazine articles related to your topic _____
6) Sending away for information about your topic _____
7) Writing your final copy _____

Part Two

Choose a specific topic in the area of transportation and write down some of the activities you would plan to do in order to create a quality piece of writing.

_____
_____
_____
_____
_____

Tip Corner

The writing process consists of: prewriting, writing, revising, editing, and publishing.

1) Prewriting: Where do you get ideas? Here are some possibilities: brainstorming, research, imagination, personal interests, memories, music, interviews, magazines, newspapers, and visual art. Other prewriting activities include journaling, free writing, making lists, visualization, mapping or clustering, outlining, and note taking

2) Writing: Write the rough draft, or rough copy. Create a working copy of your paper. It gives you something to work with. Don't censor yourself. Try to write, write, write! Let those ideas flow.

3) Revising: Ask yourself how you can improve your writing. Look at your writing with fresh eyes. Search for places where the writing could be clearer, more concise, more interesting. Is the information in the best order? Are you missing any important details? Can you improve the way you have expressed myself? Are the events in a logical order? Is each word necessary and effective? Did you use topic sentences and supporting details? Did you use a variety of strong verbs? Did you repeat any words? Did you create a mental picture of your story for the reader? Did you use a strong lead (beginning) and an effective conclusion?

4) Editing and proofreading: This stage includes checking the following: spelling grammar, capitalization, punctuation, sentence structure, subject/verb agreement, consistent verb tenses, and word usage.

5) Publishing: Share your work with others.

UNIT FOUR **CREATIVE WRITING**

Name: _____

Author's Purpose: To Persuade, Inform, or Entertain

Part One

Read each of the following and decide if the author's purpose is to:

1) persuade
2) inform
3) entertain

Tip Corner

Authors write for a number of reasons. Some authors may write nonfiction, providing true information and facts about a subject. Other authors write fiction stories, or stories that are in some way fabricated. These stories are written to entertain you. A third group of authors may write to persuade you to their way of thinking on a particular topic. Perhaps they want to prompt you to take some action as a result of reading their work.

1) I'll never forget September 7. That was the day I said good-bye to all of my good friends and moved to Steppan Hill. I saw only tears as I peered through the window of our comfortable old blue car. But by the end of the day, everything had changed. This was mostly because I came to know Emily Embers Easton. _____

2) The Robbie Radio is the best radio on the market. Even if it gets waterlogged, it will still work. It's really easy to use and will last for many years to come. The Robbie Radio only costs $19.85. Order yours today! _____

3) Be careful to stay out of the sun. The sun's rays can be very harmful to your skin and other parts of your body like your eyes. Always wear a strong sunscreen if you are going to be outside. Another good idea is to wear a long-sleeved shirt and/or pants and a wide-brimmed hat. You'll be glad you did! _____

Part Two

Choose one of the three purposes for writing: to persuade, to inform, and to entertain. Then create your own piece of writing that illustrates that purpose. Label it.

_____
_____
_____
_____
_____

UNIT FOUR **CREATIVE WRITING**

Name: _____

Characterization, Setting, and Plot

Part One

Read each sentence on the left side of the page and decide which of the three elements (characterization, setting, and plot) are present. Then match every sentence with one of the listings in the center of the page. As you can see, sometimes sentences advance both characterization and plot.

1) Emily knew when she entered the room that she was in trouble.

2) The moon shone over the island bringing light to their ancient way of life.

3) The race was to be held next week, so Jeremy had to launch his attempt right now.

4) Tyler had fought with Justin only once before.

5) Without any rain for weeks, the ground cracked, crying out for some liquid sustenance.

6) Long ago, Noah had learned to get around his mother.

7) Brandon and Kayla knew moving meant giving up everything familiar to them.

A. characterization

B. setting

C. plot

D. characterization and plot

Tip Corner

The three main elements of a story are characterization, setting, and plot.

Characters are an important part of any story. Readers often continue to read a story because they are involved with the character(s). How do readers come to know characters? They observe the way they act, speak, and think. Other characters also reveal things through their thoughts and actions.

Setting is the specific location and time that a story takes place. Sometimes this is very important to the story, and sometimes it is less important. One way to reveal the setting is to use descriptive words to help the reader to see this place in his or her mind.

Plot is the story line. Remember that a successful plot always includes some conflict or a problem.

Part Two

Write a story that includes two main characters, a specific setting, and a plot with some kind of problem.

UNIT FOUR **CREATIVE WRITING**

Name:_____

Leads (Beginnings) and Endings

Part One

Read the following leads and endings. If it sounds like a lead, write *lead* and the number of the type of lead it is (as indicated in the Tip Corner). If it sounds like an ending, just write *ending*.

1) What do you think is the most important invention ever created?

   _____

2) The first all-talking motion picture was shown in New York in 1928.

   _____

3) As I tried to outrun the huge, snarling dog, I slipped and fell. He had no problem catching up with me.

   _____

4) So we came to know that what is important is not necessarily anything you can hold in your hands.

   _____

5) "Why is it always my fault?" asked Noah sadly.

   _____

6) Ryan watched the fire from across the street. It was safer that way.

   _____

7) That situation taught me a lot. I know now to hope for the best but prepare for the worst.

   _____

Tip Corner

A good piece of writing should include a strong beginning (also called a lead) and a commendable ending. Of course, you should also try to make your middle first-rate!

There are specific techniques writers use to produce strong leads and endings. Some of the methods employed to create excellent beginnings include:

1) beginning with some action
2) starting with a question
3) beginning with an interesting fact
4) starting with dialogue
5) beginning with an anecdote (true account or story)

Here are some guidelines to produce an outstanding ending:

1) The ending should be memorable.
2) It should be brief. Tie things up in a few sentences, at most.
3) It should finish the story in a logical way.

Part Two

Choose one of the techniques for writing leads and start your own story. Indicate which type of lead you have chosen.

UNIT FOUR **CREATIVE WRITING**

Name: _____

Show, Don't Tell!

Part One

Read each of the following and decide if it is showing or telling. Write your answer on the line provided.

1) The dress was beautiful.

   _____

2) When mom brought the baby home from the hospital, I couldn't believe how little his fingers and toes were. He was so small and really, really pink. He was dressed in an outfit that would fit a doll!

   _____

3) Even though Taylor felt she knew the material, she was very nervous.

   _____

4) When I looked at the dress, it took my breath away. Pink roses and pearls were fastened to the collar and a pink ribbon circled the waist. The skirt was a billowy cloud of fabric. I felt like a princess.

   _____

5) The newborn baby was very tiny.

   _____

6) Taylor's stomach was doing flip-flops. She actually felt like she might even throw up. Her head was spinning. She tried to go over all of the material in her mind, but she couldn't remember anything. She had never been so frightened of failing.

   _____

Tip Corner

Showing, rather than telling, is a technique regularly used by professional writers. Read the following two paragraphs and see if you can discover the difference for yourself.

Example 1: When Jacob got home, he went right upstairs to his room. Even he would admit that it was a mess.

Example 2: When Jacob got home, he went right upstairs to his room. Half-eaten sandwiches lay on his bed, the floor, and his dresser. Piles of clothes were stacked in several areas of the room. Books and papers filled the desk and bookcase. The phone was buried under a pile of magazines. Empty soda cans littered the general area of the wastebasket.

Which of the two examples gives you a better picture of the story and its setting? Example 2 describes in detail what is meant by the word mess. It's much clearer in the reader's mind and much more interesting to read. In Example 1, the reader is told; in Example 2, the reader is shown.

Part Two

Choose a story idea. First, make two telling statements. Then change those telling statements into showing sentences or paragraphs.

UNIT FOUR **CREATIVE WRITING**

Name:_____

Figures of Speech

Part One
Read each of the following and decide what type of figure of speech it is. Write it down in the space provided.

1) The big, black bug bolted beyond the boy's bat.
_____

2) When I looked out the window, the people were ants.
_____

3) The snowflakes danced all the way to the ground.
_____

4) The class ate the sandwiches like a group of vultures.
_____

5) We stood in line for the tickets forever.
_____

Part Two
Create two examples each of similes, metaphors, alliteration, personification, and hyperboles.
_____
_____
_____
_____
_____
_____

Tip Corner

Figures of speech help to make writing more interesting. Here are some techniques:

Simile: Similes compare two dissimilar things using the words *like* or *as*.
Example: Melody felt that time was suddenly moving as it seems to when sitting in a dentist's chair.

Metaphor: Metaphors suggest comparisons between two dissimilar things. *Like* or *as* aren't used, but a noun must be used in the comparison.
Example: The joy she felt was a balloon lifting and swirling above the ground.

Alliteration: Alliteration is the process of repeating the same beginning sound in words that are close together.
Example: The thief tried to take tantalizing treasures.

Personification: Personification is the process of talking about a thing as if it were human.
Example: The world called to me, telling me that I should venture forth.

Hyperbole: A hyperbole is a gross overstatement.
Example: Her brother ate like a pig.

UNIT FOUR **CREATIVE WRITING**

Name: _____

Fact or Opinion

Part One

Write F if the statement is a fact or O if it is an opinion.

1) A Jack Russell terrier is the cutest breed of dog. _____
2) Dogs, cats, and birds are common pets. _____
3) Television is a waste of time. _____
4) Keeping your hands clean can help to keep you well. _____
5) Scientists have developed vaccines for chicken pox and measles. _____
6) There are 24 hours in a day. _____
7) Scientists and engineers are continually working on developing new products. _____
8) All girls like to play with dolls. _____
9) The ancient Mayan civilization spanned modern-day Mexico, Guatemala, and parts of Belize and Honduras. _____
10) If you eat too quickly, you'll be hungry again soon. _____

Tip Corner

An opinion explains how someone feels or thinks. A fact is something that can be proven to be true.

Example:

Fact: The Earth has only one sun.

Opinion: There is a man in the moon who smiles at us.

Part Two

Write one paragraph about an opinion topic. Then write another paragraph that focuses on a fact. Include supporting details.

_____
_____
_____
_____
_____

UNIT FOUR **CREATIVE WRITING**

Name: _____

Descriptive Writing

Part One

Read the following descriptive paragraph. Underline the phrases that created a picture in your mind.

In the distance we could see blue and white feathery birds enjoying the 90+ degree summer day. As they flitted from branch to branch, they had more than fun in mind. It was time to complete an important project. Their high-pitched squeals were a testament to building a nest in the nearby oak tree. Here, they would lay their baby blue eggs and wait for their family to arrive.

Part Two

Write your own descriptive paragraph. Try to appeal to the reader's senses.

> ### Tip Corner
>
> Writing descriptively means that you are able to create a picture in the mind of the reader. Often, that's because the writing appeals to the five senses: sight, smell, touch, taste, and hearing. (Descriptive paragraphs sometimes lack topic sentences.)
>
> **Example:** When my grandpa walked into the room, he smelled of the fresh lilacs he had just cut for his wife.

_____
_____
_____
_____
_____
_____
_____
_____
_____
_____
_____
_____
_____

UNIT FOUR **CREATIVE WRITING**

Name: _____

Expository Writing

Part One

Which of the following would be an example of expository writing? Circle them.

1) a poem

2) a biography

3) a report on fireflies

4) a novel

5) a journal

6) a report on Columbus

7) a haiku

8) a book report

9) a short story

10) a cartoon

Part Two

Create your own expository writing in the form of a paragraph about your favorite meal.

_____
_____
_____
_____

Tip Corner

Expository writing explains or provides information about a particular topic. A school or work report would be considered expository writing.

Once you have decided on your topic, you can use the KWL approach to complete a piece of expository writing.

K = what you already know
W = what you want or need to know
L = what you have learned

Here is one approach: Research the topic and take organized notes. Put one comment on each note card and include the source of that information. Next, read over and study your note cards and choose the fact or detail you think is most interesting. Use this as your main idea and write a topic sentence. With your main idea in mind, go back to your notes and create an outline. Then start writing a rough draft.

Example: A report on bats would be an example of expository writing.

UNIT FOUR **CREATIVE WRITING**

Name: _____

5 Ws and an H

Part One

Read the following paragraph and then answer the questions.

   This Saturday, Hozie the Clown will be hosting a special magic show dedicated to raising money for homeless families. The show will be held at the Red Roof Restaurant at 79 West Palmero Street, Kingsley, New York. Please join us and help us make this endeavor a big success!

1) Who? _____

2) What? _____

3) When? _____

4) Where? _____

5) Why? _____

6) How? _____

Part Two

Write your own story and include the five Ws and an H. Label each of them. Use additional paper if needed.

_____
_____
_____
_____

Tip Corner

The two main categories of writing are fiction and nonfiction. Fiction includes fantasies and other made-up stories. Nonfiction includes news articles and other works that are true.

Though the five Ws and an H can be effective for almost any story, they are particularly popular for use in newspaper articles. If you include all of these elements, you are giving the readers the information they seek.

Example: On Thursday, July 24, 2003, the Kids Club celebrated the opening of their hundredth recreation center in the region. Located at the corner of Pitcher and Regency Streets in Alp City, this state-of-the-art facility has a gymnasium, library, technology wing, and music and arts rooms. The money to build and furnish this center was donated by several large companies. The country's largest computer and software provider, Fast Comp, donated computers and software for the technology wing. Kids Club is a regional group of neighborhood-based facilities that provides guidance, education, and other programs for young children.

UNIT FOUR **CREATIVE WRITING**

Name: _____

Narrative Writing

Part One

Which of the following could be considered narrative writing? Circle them.

1) A story about a fantasy superhero
2) A biography of George Washington
3) A report on Lewis and Clarke
4) A poem about nature
5) A report on the Civil War
6) Your account of your last birthday
7) An actor's autobiography
8) Your account of how you acquired your pet
9) A story about an imaginary bird
10) A story about our future in space

Tip Corner

A narrative takes an actual event and tells it in a story-like fashion, either verbally or in writing. (A narrative paragraph always tells a story). Any event you write about in your life, either serious or comical, is a personal narrative.

Example: *The Diary of Anne Frank* is a personal narrative.

Part Two

Write your own personal narrative about an unusual day at school.

_____
_____
_____
_____
_____
_____
_____
_____

UNIT FOUR **CREATIVE WRITING**

Name:_____

Friendly Letters

Part One

Read the letter below and correct any mistakes.

January 22, 2004
mrs jessica marrin
st christopher, Connecticut

hello

Ive been wanting to send you a note for a long time. everything is very busy here now. mom and dad are both working long hours at the restaurant. I usually have to baby-sit with Collin and Andy after school That leaves me hardly any time to get together with friends.

I hope things get better soon.

How are you doing

Your friend sarah

Tip Corner

A friendly letter has six parts: date, address, greeting, body, closing, and signature. (Some experts recommend that you also include your return address at the top). Notice where capital letters have been used.

Example:

November 30, 2003
(1) Date
Mr. Ivan Important
777 Yucan Street
Vital Town, Illinois 60203 **(2) Address**

Dear Mr. Important, **(3) Greeting**

Body of Letter **(4) Main part** _____
_____
_____
_____
_____
_____

Love, **(5) closing**
Your name **(6) signature**

Part Two

Write a letter to a friend using the correct format. Use additional paper if needed.

UNIT FOUR **CREATIVE WRITING**

Name:_____

Poetry

Part One
There are many different kinds of poems and ways to write poems.

1) Haiku: This form of poetry originated in Japan. Each line of a haiku has a specific number of syllables.

Line 1 = 5 syllables
Line 2 = 7 syllables
Line 3 = 5 syllables

2) Format poem: Another way to write a poem is to adhere to a format. Here's one format:

Line 1 = the subject of your poem
Line 2 = list three adjectives that describe the subject
Line 3 = four *ing* words that tell things your subject does
Line 4 = three nouns that describe the subject
Line 5 = the subject again

Tip Corner
Poems often rhyme and they usually have a noticeable rhythm.

Hint: If you want to find a rhyming word without having to look in a dictionary, write out the consonants in the alphabet and put each letter in front of the word you need to rhyme (without its first letter).

3) Common rhyming poem: Poems that have lines that rhyme are most familiar to people. Perhaps Line 2 and Line 4 rhyme or any other combination of lines in the poem rhyme.

Read each of the following poems and decide whether it is a haiku, format poem, or common rhyming poem.

A)
Don't let anyone make you feel,
Less than you really are.
Hold your head high,
Aim for the sky,
And you surely will go far.

B)
Snowflakes glisten bright,
Floating gently to the ground.
A white wonderland.

C)
Dogs
Playful, cute, loyal
Jumping, romping, eating, sleeping
Friend, joy, companion
Dogs

Part Two
Choose two of the three types of poems and write your own. Use additional paper if needed.